IMAGES
of America

TWENTYNINE
PALMS

The Oasis of Mara at Twentynine Palms has been found eligible for nomination to the National Register of Historic Places. For thousands of years, it has been a sustainable source of good water in an arid environment. As a result, it played a key role in the history of the region for Native Americans. After the Gold Rush, the oasis was a natural magnet for prospectors, miners, cattlemen, and settlers who moved to the area and displaced the Native Americans from their homeland. (Photograph by Bill Houghton.)

ON THE COVER: The Oasis of Mara awaits a storm in 1940. (Photograph by Harlow Jones.)

IMAGES
of America

TWENTYNINE
PALMS

Vickie Waite, Al Gartner, and Paul F. Smith

ARCADIA
PUBLISHING

Published by Arcadia Publishing
Charleston, South Carolina

Printed in the United States of America

Library of Congress Catalog Card Number: 2006923163

For all general information contact Arcadia Publishing at:
Telephone 843-853-2070
Fax 843-853-0044
E-mail sales@arcadiapublishing.com
For customer service and orders:
Toll-Free 1-888-313-2665

Visit us on the Internet at www.arcadiapublishing.com

The City of Twentynine Palms was incorporated on November 23, 1987.

CONTENTS

ACKNOWLEDGMENTS

We offer our sincere thanks to the Twentynine Palms Historical Society, its board of directors, and the volunteers at the Old Schoolhouse Museum for providing access to their historical photographs. Unless otherwise noted, all photographs in this book were provided by the Twentynine Palms Historical Society. We express our gratitude to Bob and Edith Carter; Jeff Dunn; Cheryl Erickson; Art Kidwell; Don Malone; Ginny Salisbury; Robert Smeaton; Dianna Stevens, who founded the historical society, and to Gene Ludwig, under whose leadership the Old Schoolhouse was moved and renovated into a museum.

We personally wish to thank Marion Gartner, who has been with this project from the start, offering invaluable comments, helping organize the photographs, and meticulously proofreading the material. Thanks also to Melanie Spoo and Jan Sabala, museum curators at Joshua Tree National Park headquarters in Twentynine Palms, for sharing images from their Campbell and Keys collections and Jim Wharff for his gold mining expertise.

We are especially grateful for those early photographers whose images provide a rare glimpse into our area's history, including Eddie Adams, Burton Frasher, George A. Grant, Bill Hatch, E. N. James, Harlow Jones, Derald Martin, Ted Richardson, Maud Russell, Robert Van Lahr, and the many unidentified photographers who recorded the early growth of Twentynine Palms. Special thanks also go to descendents of the pioneer families, including Jim Bagley, Jack Grover, Gene Kenney, Elizabeth (Hatch) Meyer, Jane (Van Lahr) Smith, and others who shared private collections for this project; to the Underhill family and Kelly O'Sullivan at the *Desert Trail* for their newspaper records and assistance; and to the families who have donated their photographs to the historical society, without which this book would not have been possible.

Early historians Maud Russell, Hazel Spell, and Harold and Lucile Weight deserve gratitude for their documentation of the early times, as do authors Helen Bagley, Elizabeth Campbell, Art Kidwell, Lulu Rasmussen O'Neal, Pat Rimmington, and Joan Wilson. Without them, our community's history might have been dust in the wind.

Finally, thanks to Jane Smith, Steve Brown, and Tollian and Sarah Waite for their support of our work.

INTRODUCTION

This is an invitation to visit a land that was baptized by geology and climate. We will introduce the adventurers who were drawn to this area by those attractions. They stayed to make their own personal histories of frontier survival and pioneer homesteads in the vast Mojave Desert outback and Joshua Tree National Park, one of the premier national parks in the great American West.

Chapter one begins the story with the founding of Joshua Tree National Park. In the 1920s, Minerva Hoyt of Pasadena, California, was appalled by the massive theft of desert cactus in the California desert. She did more than just complain about it. She organized a careful campaign to persuade Pres. Franklin Roosevelt and his New Deal Administration to set aside a large national monument that would protect over one million acres of land from horticultural predators from the cities. She was a formidable and persuasive person. Roosevelt listened to Minerva, and on August 10, 1936, he signed a presidential proclamation setting aside 825,430 acres as Joshua Tree National Monument. It became a national park by act of Congress in 1994.

Geology is the natural dictator of the history that takes place in any area. Chapter two describes how the tectonic action of major earthquakes over 9,000 years ago created an oasis of water and food for early peoples in the desert. Not much is known about these adventurers, but Twentynine Palms archaeologists William and Elizabeth Campbell were able to discover and record their presence and style of living in the deserts surrounding the Twentynine Palms community.

Chapter three explores the lives of people who lived at the Oasis of Mara from the mid-1850s to modern times. They were risk takers. Even today, a road sign on the east end of Twentynine Palms announces "100 MILES TO THE NEXT SERVICES." This was the last stop, and it took courage to come and settle here. Mentioned in this chapter are historic Chemehuevi and Serrano Indians, early cattlemen, settlers who came for their health, and the birth of tourism at the internationally known 29 Palms Inn. This chapter will also share newly discovered details of the infamous Willie Boy incident of September 1909.

Chapter four introduces pioneer Bill Keys. He came to Twentynine Palms in 1910 when it was a many-days journey from supplies and law and order. He acquired mining interests, built an ore-processing gold mill, and took over the frontier Desert Queen Ranch where he and his wife, Frances, raised a family. Keys was a rough-and-ready guy. He joined Teddy Roosevelt's Rough Riders and was a close acquaintance of Death Valley Scotty. You will learn of several of his dangerous Wild West adventures in Twentynine Palms, including a showdown with Homer Urton and a shoot-out to the death with retired deputy Worth Bagley. Keys was an excellent shot, and Worth Bagley did not survive the gunfight.

Chapter five tells the story of the forgotten gold rush of Twentynine Palms. For more than 50 years, gold mining was the center of action in Twentynine Palms. Gold was free for the taking, and these early prospectors could not resist the possibility of finding sudden wealth merely by looking for it in the dirt and rocks of the desert. This chapter visits the Lost Horse Mine; travels with Frank Sabathe on his freighting wagon to the Dale Mining District; illustrates the Chilcots and Benitos at the Blue Bell Mine; and introduces Bill McHaney, who came to the area in 1879.

Eagle Eye McFarland serenaded at the Dirty Sock Camp, and a photograph shows Jack Meek, a legendary miner, lawman, gunman, and colorful character, bragging about some ore samples obtained with the help of his prospector friend Les Spell.

Chapter six shows daily lives of important early settlers in Twentynine Palms, including Bill Smith, who arrived to start a homestead in an old truck with $1.34 in his pocket and a broken arm. Other early photographs depict the eastern-style mansion of the Campbells, the important works of the Hatch family, and some of the early Stubbs brothers' adobe buildings. Dr. James Luckie, the "Father of Twentynine Palms," ushered the town into a new era when he brought respiratory victims from World War I to Twentynine Palms for their health.

Every town must have a store and surrounding business community. Chapter seven depicts the start of business at the Bagley Store and Plaza on Adobe Road. The year was 1927. Streetcars and automobiles were already congesting the streets of Los Angeles. But here in the desert it was a different story. This chapter introduces the Bagley family, their neighbors and other families, and the Tom Mix Straight Shooters Club.

Although Twentynine Palms was a small community, it actually had two different business centers. Chapter eight shows the Four Corners area and its small businesses. Pictured are Dean's Coffee Shop, the 29 Palms Village land sales office, Ada Hatch stranded in her Model A in the middle of a desert flash flood, and the way the dirt road into town looked in 1933. The first bank, market, drugstore, and survey office provide a sense of what it was like to live and work in Twentynine Palms in these early days. The pioneer spirit was demonstrated by John and Clara Dobler, who initiated a daily trek all the way to Riverside and back to supply the community with fresh dairy products in the early 1950s. Their son, Conrad Dobler, inherited that toughness and went on to a professional football career where he was widely known as the "Meanest Man in Pro Football."

Starting in the 1920s, Twentynine Palms slowly began to acquire schools, churches, a police officer who patrolled the desert by air, a hospital, post office, art galleries, newspaper, bus service, and a museum. Chapter nine illustrates how all of these community services began. The people provided their services when they did not have much money and when they were located many miles from larger, urban civilizations. These were bootstrap efforts.

Bold, adventurous people usually know how to have a good time. Twentynine Palms was no exception. Chapter 10 introduces the social scene, rodeos, parades, jalopy races on the dry lake beds, and an old-fashioned drive-in movie. Actress Esther Williams, who served as honorary mayor of Twentynine Palms in 1948, and Academy Award–winning songwriter Allie Wrubel are also pictured.

Time and space did not permit the introduction of all the important historic people of Twentynine Palms. So, when visiting the community, be sure to stop by Joshua Tree National Park's Oasis Visitor Center, the Old Schoolhouse Museum of the Twentynine Palms Historical Society, and the many artists' studios and galleries in the area. They will introduce other pioneers, old and new, who took part in the history of the area and came to love the unique scenery and wildlife of Joshua Tree National Park, the wild natural beauty of the Mojave Desert, and the friendly community spirit of Twentynine Palms.

One

TWENTYNINE PALMS AND JOSHUA TREE NATIONAL PARK

In 1936, when the country's Depression was in full swing, something exciting was happening in Twentynine Palms. After many years of lobbying in California and Washington, D.C., Minerva Hamilton Hoyt persuaded Pres. Franklin D. Roosevelt to sign a presidential proclamation establishing Joshua Tree National Monument. Its headquarters and visitor center would eventually be established at the Oasis of Mara in Twentynine Palms. After receiving national park status in 1994, this popular destination for rock climbers, hikers, campers, artists, and photographers saw an increase in the number of annual visitors to 1.4 million. (Postcard by Harlow Jones, 1943.)

Minerva Hamilton Hoyt had a passion for stopping the widespread destruction of desert cacti and Joshua trees by vandals and collectors. An expert on desert vegetation, this Pasadena socialite founded the International Desert Conservation League for desert protection and played a pivotal role in the creation of Joshua Tree National Monument in 1936. It was hard to say no to this persuasive and energetic woman. (Courtesy of the Hoyt family.)

In 1994, Pres. William J. Clinton signed the Desert Protection Act, which changed Joshua Tree National Monument into Joshua Tree National Park with 794,000 acres. Above, at park headquarters in Twentynine Palms on the 10th anniversary of this enhanced, protected status, park superintendent Curt Sauer and chief of interpretation Joe Zarki display a handsome plaque received from the Basin Wide Foundation that honors the achievement of Minerva Hoyt.

Three generations of Minerva Hamilton Hoyt's family traveled to Twentynine Palms to celebrate Joshua Tree National Park's 10th anniversary and the dedication of a mural honoring their ancestor who played the key role in establishing the original Joshua Tree National Monument in 1936.

Scenic Joshua Tree National Park has been a popular backyard destination for Twentynine Palms residents for years. Here homesteaders William B. "Bill" and Ada Hatch lead friends on a 1933 picnic and sightseeing adventure in Hidden Valley. (Courtesy of the Hatch collection.)

The caption on this photograph reads, "Circa 1936–37—Bagley Picnic in Indian Cove. Pictured are Stan Krushat, John Bagley, Ben Steeg, Art Krushat, Ethyl Olsen, George Michels, Al Curry, Maude Martin, Betty Michels, Helen Bagley, Florence Curry, Bess Flickinger, Jimmy McCullum, Tom Martin, Frank Bagley, Herb Tower, Heine Olsen, Ray Flickinger, Rick Cain, Edith Mildred Michels, Alma Steeg, Olive Krushat, Sara Krushat, Dona Tower, and Chuck Martin." (Photograph by Lester Krushat.)

The dramatic scenery of Joshua Tree National Park has drawn visitors to Twentynine Palms for over 100 years. (Photograph by Harlow Jones.)

Two

SEARCH FOR THE
BEGINNING
WHO WAS HERE FIRST?

This early photograph of the Oasis of Mara at Twentynine Palms shows its towering Washingtonia filifera palm trees in the dry Mojave Desert. They can be seen from many miles away and tell a story of available water and natural food supplies. The Oasis of Mara most likely supported villages of desert peoples and animals for thousands of years. Commonly asked questions by visitors to the site today are, "How long has this natural oasis been here?" "Who lived here first?" (Photograph by Burton Frasher.)

In 2003, geologist Ana Cadena from the University of Central Washington directed an excavation at the Oasis of Mara. Working with San Diego State University, she looked for evidence of the age and frequency of major earthquake events along the Pinto Mountain Fault in Twentynine Palms. The trench was 220 feet long, 12 to 15 feet deep, and 3 feet wide. Geologists, archaeologists, biologists, and historians were surprised by her findings.

Geologist Ana Cadena points out a 3-foot-thick zone of organic deposits from a sag pond formed more than 9,000 years ago as a result of fault activity. A remnant of that pond exists at the 29 Palms Inn today, where the Oasis of Mara has long been a site for water and rich biological resources. In the late 1920s and 1930s, pioneer archaeologists William and Elizabeth Campbell of Twentynine Palms located many early man sites in the area, confirming human occupation of several thousand years.

Elizabeth W. Crozer Campbell and her husband, William Campbell, camped at the Oasis of Mara during the winter of 1924–1925. They came here on the recommendation of Dr. James B. Luckie of Pasadena, California, who treated William for the effects of mustard gas suffered during World War I. Enjoying the benefits of clean, desert air, his health improved, and the couple decided to homestead in Twentynine Palms. (Courtesy of Joshua Tree National Park.)

William H. Campbell holds a Native American *olla* he discovered on an archaeological expedition. He was known as "Lucky Bill" for his instinct for finding Native American artifacts. The Campbell homestead in Twentynine Palms housed many catalogued pieces and was the Desert Branch of the Southwest Museum of Los Angeles. Much of this collection is now at the Joshua Tree National Park curatorial facility and displayed in the park's Oasis Visitor Center. (Courtesy of Joshua Tree National Park.)

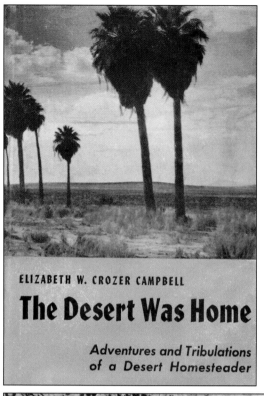

ELIZABETH W. CROZER CAMPBELL

The Desert Was Home

**Adventures and Tribulations
of a Desert Homesteader**

Elizabeth Campbell authored a colorful book on early life in the frontier community of Twentynine Palms. *The Desert Was Home*, published in 1961, chronicles their arrival at the oasis in 1924, their adventuresome forays into the surrounding desert, their challenges in building a house on a 160-acre homestead, and their role in the pioneer spirit that built a community. Elizabeth died in Twentynine Palms in 1971.

One of many desert camping adventures of William and Elizabeth Campbell is pictured. While they traveled in high camping style, they were serious scientists who were not afraid to kneel in caves and sift through ancient dust searching for clues to early lives of Native Americans. They acquired many clues to important collecting sites from their longtime friendship with William McHaney, a prospector and early resident of the Oasis of Mara.

The Campbells and their workers are pictured in the early 1930s, taking a lunch break at one of their excavation sites. Their work in Late-Pleistocene and Holocene sites in the Pinto Basin of what is now Joshua Tree National Park and Lake Mojave are treated as breakthrough advances in North American archaeology. Their work is referenced in almost all significant publications dealing with early human occupation in the West.

"Lucky Bill" and an associate are searching for evidence in a dig. The Campbells worked with scientists from other disciplines in their research. University geologists helped them determine the chronology of water levels in now dry lake beds that helped establish the ages of human settlements around those ancient lakeshores. The Campbells were the first to describe the Pinto and the Lake Mojave projectile points at these desert water sources.

Working out of their headquarters in Twentynine Palms, William and Elizabeth Campbell carefully surveyed the caves and rock outcrops in the surrounding mountains. They located these spirit sticks guarding the entrance to one of the caves. (Courtesy of Joshua Tree National Park.)

The Campells found these early Native American *ollas*, age unknown, in a rock overhang. Specimens like these are carefully preserved at Joshua Tree National Park, and someday scientists may be able to apply techniques for discovering their age, use, and origin. Elizabeth Campbell was a nationally known scholar and writer. Her scientific writings appeared in publications of the Southwest Museum and the professional journals *American Antiquity* and *Science*. (Courtesy of Joshua Tree National Park.)

Three

THE PEOPLE
OF THE OASIS

In 1856, government surveyor A. P. Green visited the Oasis of Mara at Twentynine Palms and commented, "There are some large palm trees from which the springs take their name . . . There are some Indian huts in Section Thirty-three. The Indians use the leaf of the palm tree for making baskets, hats, etc. Around the springs there is a growth of cane of which the Indians make bows for their arrows." At the time of Green's visit, he likely encountered the Serrano Indians. In the late 1860s, a small band of Chemehuevi migrated to the oasis after fighting with the Mohaves along the Colorado River. (Chemehuevis, Lithograph by H. B. Mollhausen, Ives Expedition, 1858.)

This picture of Chemehuevi basket makers was taken in 1897 at the west end of the oasis at Twentynine Palms. Euro-Americans had arrived and were living nearby. The Chemehuevi were well respected for their farming and basket-weaving skills. However, note the look of apprehension on the faces of these women. In order to survive the American invasion, they knew they must learn to assimilate into this new culture or face extinction. The question was how? They were not allowed to testify in court and would not become citizens until 1925. Their 160-acre reservation to the south was without water and offered little of the substance of life. But they survived, and their descendants now have another reservation near Indio with a successful casino business operation—Spotlight 29 Casino. (Courtesy of Joshua Tree National Park.)

The Indian Service first visited the Native American village at Twentynine Palms in 1909. Shown here are, from left to right, Indian Service officer W. F. "Pussyfoot" Johnson; Chuck Warren of Warren's Well; Native American superintendent Clara True; Horace Bryan; and Mary, Horace's sister, both from Redlands. Superintendent True would attempt to move the Native Americans to other reservations in Palms Springs, Banning, and Mission Creek. (Photograph by Maud Russell.)

This 1909 photograph shows, from left to right, officer Pussyfoot Johnson; Jim Pine, tribal leader; Pine's wife, Matilda; and Constable Ben de Crevecoeur. Indian superintendent Clara True reported that the Pine family did not want to move to another reservation. The oasis was their homeland, and the cemetery held the remains of their children. Within months, the Willie Boy incident would eliminate their chances to stay. (Photograph by Maud Russell.)

Arrest for Double Murder

San Bernardino, Cal., Oct. 5, 1909

Willie Boy

A Chimehuevis Indian. 26 years old, about 5 feet, 10 inches in height; slim built, walks and stands erect; yellowish complexion, sunken cheeks; high cheek bones; talks good English with a drawl; has a scar under chin where he has been shot and some teeth gone. For years lived about Victorville, with a halfbreed American woman with two children, a girl of 10 and a boy of 2 years. She left him because he had beaten her, and returned to Victorville. His people living among the Kingston mountains, along the Nevada state line. He killed Mike Boniface, at Banning on the night of Sunday, September 26, and Ioleta Boniface, at The Pipes, in San Bernardino county, September 30.

An Indian filling the description of Willie Boy was seen cooking a rabbit between Goffs Station and Manvel on Sunday evening, October 3rd. When he saw the approaching parties he ran away. This might have been Willie Boy as his mother was at Vanderbilt a short time ago.

J. C. RALPHS, Sheriff.

Found dead Oct. 15-09.

This wanted poster tells of the Willie Boy incident from the Euro-American perspective. Willie Boy lived at the oasis in Twentynine Palms. He was in love with Carlota, who was also known as Ioleta or Lolita, the daughter of William Mike (Mike Boniface), whose family also lived there. They were related and thus forbidden to marry.

Chemehuevi Indian tracker Segundo Chino was a friend of William Mike. On September 26, 1909, Willie Boy shot William Mike and escaped on foot into the desert with Mike's daughter Carlota. Over the next few weeks, several posses were formed, including one with Joe Touain, Charlie Reche, Ben De Crevecoeur, and Ben's brother Waldemar. Carlota was shot and killed. Willie Boy, a well-known Chemehuevi runner, outraced the posses for almost three weeks.

The posse claimed to have found Willie Boy's body on October 15, 1909, ostensibly having committed suicide with his last bullet. Reporter and photographer Randolph Madison of the *Los Angeles Record* took this photograph of the alleged body of Willie Boy. Native American members of the posse supposedly cremated the body. No close-up picture was ever taken.

Seven months after the Willie Boy incident, Pussyfoot Johnson, Ben De Crevecoeur, Mary Gray Arnold from the U.S. Indian School, and Henry Pablo, Native American policeman at Morongo Reservation, returned to Twentynine Palms. Most of the Native Americans had left the Oasis of Mara. They feared white violence against them, and the Indian Service removed the remaining Native Americans from their home in Twentynine Palms. (Photograph by Maud Russell.)

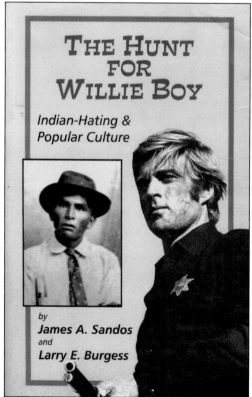

Historians James Sandos, Larry Burgess, and Clifford Trafzer studied the Willie Boy incident in the 1990s. They discovered evidence that Carlota was killed by a posse member, probably accidentally. Willie Boy was not a drunken, violent-prone Native American. He likely killed William Mike accidentally. Willie Boy did not commit suicide but escaped across the desert, stayed with relatives in the Old Woman Mountains, and probably died in Las Vegas in the late 1920s.

24

Paulino Weaver was the first Anglo-American to visit the Oasis of Mara. He had traveled with Ewing Young's trapping expedition to California in 1831, and in the mid-1850s, Weaver found a secret route from his home in the San Gorgonio Pass through the Morongo Basin to the Colorado River, stopping at the oasis in Twentynine Palms where he watered and fed his cattle before heading on the long, dry stretch to the east. Thirty years later, pioneer Bill McHaney described the saltbushes and galletta grass as growing up to the bellies of grazing cows.

By 1898, nearly 1,000 men were prospecting for gold east of the oasis in the Dale Mining District, and the population surge brought cattle, horses, and burros to the oasis for water and grazing. This 1902 photograph of the oasis reflects the damage done to natural vegetation by the men and animals that converged on the area where saltbushes and galletta grass once grew abundantly. (Photograph by E. N. James.)

This 1902 photograph shows the old road to the Oasis of Mara. In 1888, Dr. J. W. Hazlet noted, "Here in the middle of a vast sand desert is one of the finest cold-water springs I have ever had the good fortune to see and taste." (Photograph by E. N. James.)

The Old Adobe at the oasis, seen here in 1915, was built about 1890 by a Mr. Aldridge of Santa Ana with help from Billy Neaves. The building stood until 1947 and served as a health resort for Aldridge, a horse-changing station, a real estate office, an office for Pinto Basin Subdividers, headquarters for Barker and Shay cattlemen, a residence for prospectors, and temporary lodging for families homesteading in Twentynine Palms. (Courtesy of Pat Rimmington.)

Here is a 1902 photograph of Chuckwalla "Quartz" Wilson's home at the oasis, which included tunnels burrowed into the side of the hill. Wilson filed mining claims in the region and was reported to have discovered the El Dorado Mine and been a codiscoverer of the Virginia Dale Mine in 1885. Wilson arrived in Twentynine Palms in 1883. Although he found many successful claims, he died penniless. (Photograph by E. N. James.)

In this grave located along the nature trail at Joshua Tree National Park's Oasis Visitor Center rests Maria Eleanor Whallon. Only 18 years old, she was traveling with her mother, who was moving to the Eaton Mine in the Dale District for a new job as camp cook. Maria suffered from tuberculosis and hoped that life in the desert would be her cure. She didn't make it. On March 10, 1903, she died at the oasis after a long, rough trip on a horse-drawn freighter from Banning.

William 'Bill" McHaney and brother James moved from Missouri to the Big Bear area in 1875. Accused of rustling cattle, they were ousted from Big Bear. Bill arrived at the oasis in Twentynine Palms in 1879 and lived there and in outlying locations in Music Valley and the Desert Queen Ranch until his death in 1937. He outlived his unsavory past and became a respected resident.

In the early 1900s, this gold mill and ore-processing operation was located at the Oasis of Mara, where it could take advantage of the plentiful supply of water.

The Gold Park Hotel was built by E. E. Chapman between 1923 and 1926 at the east end of the oasis. He acquired the property from speculator Alfred Violette, who had purchased it from Southern Pacific Land Company in 1922. Chapman was discouraged when a proposed highway through Twentynine Palms did not materialize. He sold the property in 1926 to William Roberts. This photograph shows a Roberts family member at the hotel around 1926.

This photograph taken about 1926 of Gold Park Hotel shows five hotel rooms on the right and the dining room and owners' living quarters on the left. Gold Park had five other rooms and four cottages, one of which was used as a school. The hotel also operated a grocery store, gas station, and post office. In 1928, Roberts moved the hotel to the west end of the oasis and renamed it 29 Palms Inn.

In early 1929, Harry Johansing, an optimistic and successful Los Angeles businessman, joined with David Faries to form the Twentynine Palms Corporation, with lesser partners C. Gratton Fitzgerald and a Mr. Kingston. Johansing and his wife, Millie, are pictured here in the early 1930s. The company bought the 29 Palms Inn and 480 acres from Roberts. They intended to subdivide the property and sell lots to the public, but the Depression put an end to their sales promotion.

This adobe bungalow was one of several built for the 29 Palms Inn in 1934 by the Stubbs brothers, who had learned the art of building with local adobe materials. In about 1938, Harry Johansing and David Faries divided their holdings and liquidated the Twentynine Palms Corporation. Faries got most of their raw land, and Johansing received the oasis with the 29 Palms Inn and some of the nearby acreage.

In 1929, Harry and Millie Johansing asked their daughter, Mary Claire, and her husband, Robert "Bob" Van Lahr, to come to Twentynine Palms to sell real estate. When that didn't prove profitable, the Van Lahrs took over the operation of the 29 Palms Inn. In this early 1940s picture, Bob Van Lahr is milking the family goat while Mary Claire and their daughters, Ann, Mary, and Jane, look on.

This early photograph shows Bob Van Lahr in the 29 Palms Inn kitchen preparing to butcher a side of lamb. In the 1940s, Twentynine Palms was a long distance from restaurant supply companies. Van Lahr made frequent trips to Banning and even as far away as Los Angeles to get fresh meat and produce for the inn restaurant. The arrival of Dobler's Hi-Desert Food Service in the 1950s made life easier for local restaurants.

This photograph, taken *c.* 1946, shows Jane Van Lahr enjoying the early morning sun on top of one of the adobe walls at the 29 Palms Inn. In 1977, Jane and her family purchased the inn from her parents, Bob and Mary Claire Van Lahr. She has been the family innkeeper ever since.

The 29 Palms Inn is seen here as it enters the postwar era in 1946. The inn has since become a popular destination resort for entertainment industry personalities, writers, artists, amateur and professional photographers, and a new generation of desert wilderness fans who visit Joshua Tree National Park. (Photograph by Harlow Jones.)

Four

BILL KEYS AND DESERT QUEEN RANCH

The Desert Queen Ranch was established by the McHaney brothers in the mid-1890s in Queen Valley, located in the mountains south of Twentynine Palms, and is now a popular tourist attraction in Joshua Tree National Park. Bill and Jim McHaney used the ranch while they ran cattle in the area and operated the nearby Desert Queen Mine. They built a few cabins, a large adobe barn, and a five-stamp crushing mill for processing gold ore. When the McHaneys left the ranch, it was operated by Frederick Morgan, a mining promoter from Pasadena.

This photograph from the early 1900s shows the original barn built by the McHaneys at Desert Queen Ranch about 1894 and the primitive wagons used for hauling and transportation at that time. (Courtesy of Willis Keys.)

William F. "Bill" Keys, born in 1879, left Nebraska at 15 to pursue careers in mining, ranching, as a member of Teddy Roosevelt's Rough Riders, and as deputy sheriff of Mojave County in Arizona. He came to Twentynine Palms in about 1910 and worked with Frederick Morgan as assayer and caretaker at the Desert Queen Mine. When Morgan died, Keys filed on the property in 1916–1917 for unpaid back wages and became the new owner. He acquired additional properties in the area under the federal homestead laws.

Barker and Shay cowboys are seen here in 1914 grazing cattle near Desert Queen Ranch. Some of the homestead properties acquired by Bill Keys included lands used by cattle ranchers C. O. Barker and William Shay. Shay was related to San Bernardino County sheriff Walter Shay, and Keys experienced difficulty with them over the years. (Courtesy of Robert "Doc" Smeton.)

Homer Urton was a Barker and Shay cowpuncher who had a long-running dispute with Bill Keys over trespassing and cattle ownership. One day, Urton made a deliberate trespass through Desert Queen Ranch, and Keys went looking for him. At the confrontation, Urton drew his gun, and Keys shot him in the arm. The sheriff arrested Keys. After a lengthy trial, Keys was acquitted on the basis of testimony from witnesses that the shooting was self-defense.

Travel to and from the ranch in 1918 was likely uncomfortable for Bill Keys's wife, Frances, seated in the front wagon. Keys described a typical journey in a 1966 interview: "Well, they would make from Banning down to Whitewater the first day, and then from Whitewater to Warren's Ranch, Morongo, the second day, then to Warren's Well (Yucca Valley) the third day and Quail Springs the fourth day and this here the fifth day." (Courtesy of Willis Keys.)

Bill Keys's Desert Queen Ranch was a long distance from town, and the early pioneers in the area established their own one-room school at the ranch. Shown in 1928 are students (first row) Don McRoberts and Phyllis Keys with her dog; (second row, standing) Pat Keys and Marion Headington.

The desert country around the Desert Queen Ranch required a rugged vehicle with hard metal wheels that could withstand the sharp rocks and cactus spines. In this 1935 photograph, Bill Keys is shown driving his 1910 Chase vehicle, with his friend Charley Wise in the front seat. Wise was a mule skinner and prospector. (Courtesy of Willis Keys.)

Desert Queen Ranch was many miles from spare parts and fancy equipment. Bill Keys was skilled at adapting available machinery and fabricating what he needed to get the job done. Here is his Fordson tractor when it was rigged to power a large saw blade for cutting wood. Keys was a collector of used hardware and equipment, wherever it could be found, for use at the ranch. (Courtesy of Charles Teel.)

Bill Keys' neighbor, Worth Bagley, had threatened Keys for traveling on a disputed road from Desert Queen Ranch to his Wall Street Mill. On May 11, 1942, he ambushed Keys along that road, but Keys shot Bagley dead. It was clearly self-defense, but Bagley was retired from the sheriff's department, which had a long-standing antagonism toward Keys. Keys served five years in prison before Erle Stanley Gardner and others found new evidence supporting his pardon in 1956.

Bill and Frances Keys, seen here in 1950, hosted many visitors at Desert Queen Ranch and made many friends. Frances Lawton met Bill Keys while working as a stenographer and at Western Union in Los Angeles. She raised a family on the ranch and was an excellent cook and gardener. Her son Willis states that she could fix anything from steaks and gravy to pancakes, garden vegetables, jackrabbit, and cottontail.

Five

THE FORGOTTEN GOLD RUSH

While the California Gold Rush of 1849 was well known throughout the world, little was written about the "forgotten gold rush" in the desert areas of Southern California. Colorful characters left the "easy pickings" up north and filed mining claims in what is now Joshua Tree National Park. This prospector's cabin in Gold Park was said to be home to a Hindu mystic from Alaska for 21 years. The site was one of many remaining cabins, mill sites, and mining operations documented in October 1941 by National Park Service photographer George A. Grant. (Courtesy of Pete Malone.)

Bill McHaney, a respected desert miner, is pictured at his camp in Music Valley southeast of the oasis at Twentynine Palms in February 1928. McHaney came to the Morongo Basin in 1879 and to the Twentynine Palms area around 1888. He was the first permanent settler and a good friend of the local Native Americans, who showed him where to find water, trails, and gold mines. (Courtesy of William A. Roberts.)

"Eagle Eye" McFarland is shown here at the Dirty Sock Mining Camp at County Well on the road from Indio to Twentynine Palms about 1912. The camp was named for the old socks miners often used to strain mercury-gold amalgam when they lacked a proper chamois filter. (Courtesy of Joshua Tree National Park.)

Freighting supplies from Banning to the Dale Mining District, east of Twentynine Palms, took three to four days of hard driving over little more than desert ruts with a stopover at the oasis. In the late 1800s and early 1900s, Frank Sabathe hauled supplies with this freighting team and later operated a stage from his homestead in Amboy. (Photograph by Maud Russell.)

Lost Horse Mine was one of the richest gold mines in the desert and is now in Joshua Tree National Park. Frank Diebold, who, afraid of nearby outlaws, sold his claim to Johnny Lang for $1,000, possibly discovered the mine. Lang and his partners filed on the claim in 1893. In 1895–1896, they sold their interests to the Ryans, who installed a 10-stamp mill. More than 9,000 ounces of gold were extracted before 1900.

Frank Sabathe, prospector and miner, came to Twentynine Palms in 1892. He filed on 14 claims in the Dale Mining District, and to get supplies, he bought a 10-horse team and began hauling supplies from Banning 90 miles away. He hauled for other miners as well, charging $30 a ton, and went into the freighting business. (Photograph by Robert Van Lahr.)

Phil Sullivan (right), who came to Twentynine Palms in 1898, furnishes fiddle music for the boys in this 1924 photograph. Sullivan had an interest in the Anaconda and other desert mines and was a partner in the Taylor Sullivan Mining Company formed in 1907. Sullivan Road in Twentynine Palms is named after him and was the main road into town until Highway 62 was established. (Courtesy of George V. Michels.)

F. L. Botsford (left) visits longtime Dale and Pinto district miner Jack Meek in this photograph dated March 22, 1947. As a youth, Botsford worked with his father at the Brooklyn Mine. He returned to the area in the 1940s seeking mining stories for historian Maud Russell.

A young Robert Michels (middle row, left) rides through a dry Morongo Canyon in 1918 with his family, including the senior Michels, George Columbus and Elizabeth, and the Geils family. Brother George Michels homesteaded 160 acres in 1921 southeast of what is now Utah Trail and Amboy Road. The following year he brought his bride, Mildred.

Prospectors Les Spell (left) and Jack Meek show their gold ore to pioneer druggist Edward Kenney in the late 1940s. Spell, the son of a Colorado mining family, came to Twentynine Palms in 1926, worked in numerous mines, and was foreman at the Gold Crown, Nightingale, and Carlyle Mines. In the 1950s, Spell wrote a regular column on mining for the *Desert Trail* newspaper. (Courtesy of Margaret Kenney.)

Jack Meek's mining camp, known as Meek's Center, is documented here in 1941 by National Park Service photographer George A. Grant. Meek had a reputation as lawman, gunman, miner, and all-around colorful character in Twentynine Palms from the 1920s until his death in 1951. He operated mines in the Dale District, including the Jack Meek East Group and the Desert King Mine. (Courtesy of Pete Malone.)

At the Blue Bell Mine in 1937 are, from left to right, Owen and Ernie Chilcot and Clovis and Mary Benito. The Benitos were homesteaders who arrived in 1927. After a failed poultry business in the Pinto Basin, they won a bid in 1930 to deliver mail from Whitewater to Twentynine Palms, a service they operated for 10 years, and additionally opened a grocery store on the corner of Adobe and Sullivan Roads. Clovis operated the store, service station, and garage, while Mary and the children delivered the mail.

A prospector's cabin at the Desert Queen Mine, in what is now Joshua Tree National Park, is seen on October 2, 1941. This rich gold mine was discovered by Frank James in 1904 and maintained until his violent death; the mine then ended up in the hands of the McHaney brothers. William F. "Bill" Keys was the last owner. (Photograph by George A. Grant, National Park Service.)

Prospector Eloge "Frenchie" Auclair and the Golden Bee Mill are seen here on October 6, 1941. The mill was located near the vertical shaft of the Golden Bee Mine on the north flank of the Hexie Mountains, now in Joshua Tree National Park. (Photograph by George A. Grant, National Park Service.)

The new Gold Crown Mine, also known as the Lorman, seen in 1941, overlooks Dale Dry Lake and the Sheephole Mountains in the distance. The property, taken over by the Gold Crown Mining Company of Los Angeles in the 1930s, was equipped with a 60-ton ball mill in 1937. (Photograph by George A. Grant, National Park Service.)

Old Dale declined when operations moved to New Dale in 1900. Located east of Twentynine Palms about 15 miles on what is now Highway 62, the site was chosen because water could be found near the surface, and water was essential for the hundreds of placer miners who were working throughout the district in the 1880s. Old Dale was at its height in 1898–1899 with a population of about 70. (Photograph by Harlow Jones.)

Jonathan "Quartz" Wilson, who lived at the Twentynine Palms oasis, and Tom Lyon discovered Virginia Dale Mine in about 1885. The remains of the site are pictured in 1941. Water was pumped five miles from the Old Dale well, in the area that became known as the Dale Mining District. (Photograph by George A. Grant, National Park Service.)

This 1913 photograph of the general store in New Dale shows women and children living amidst the rough environment of the Dale Mining District at Twentynine Palms. Mrs. Ike Reed (left), whose husband was Dale Judicial Township justice of the peace, and Jeanne Sabathe, whose husband, Frank, was a freighter, are seen here with their children. The boy in the center is believed to be Dale Sabathe, the first child born in Dale. (Courtesy of Robert Van Lahr collection.)

The Bill Keys five-stamp gold mill from the Gold Queen Mine in Lost Horse Valley is featured in this 1941 photograph. Early Twentynine Palms homesteader Ed Malone is pictured on the left. (Courtesy of Pete Malone.)

Gold miners crushed and processed ore in an *arrastra*, like this abandoned Jack Meek *arrastra* seen at Old Dale in 1941. A large rock or other grinding tool was dragged by mules around the *arrastra* to pulverize gold-bearing rocks, which were then washed to separate the gold. (Photograph by George A. Grant, National Park Service.)

When miner Karl Schapel's cabin burned in 1961, 300 residents of Twentynine Palms showed up to rebuild his home. Seen here are, from left to right, Betty Fields, Karl Schapel, Gen. Louis Fields, Sally and Bill Ince, John and Barbara Hilton, Blanche Ellis, and Grace and Victor Kingman. Schapel filed on a claim purchased from Jack Meek in 1940, opened the Golden Egg Mine, and enjoyed showing visitors his mining operation. (Photograph by Bill Hatch.)

When cattleman Johnny Lang tracked a wandering horse into the mountains in 1893, he supposedly found gold ore, and the Lost Horse Mine was born. By 1896, he was accused of skimming profits, and he lost his mining partners Ed Holland, James J. Fife, and his father, George Lang. When new partners James and Thomas Ryan caught him stealing, he was forced to sell out. Lang died in 1926 and is buried in Lost Horse Valley.

Gold ore processor, miner, cattleman, and homesteader William F. "Bill" Keys, accompanied by family and friends, drove his "Keysmobile" in the 1940 Pioneer Days Parade. This iron-wheeled truck was originally built by the Chase Company in 1910 for the Paymaster Mine and was later modified by Keys for use at his Desert Queen Mine and ranch in what is now Joshua Tree National Park. (Courtesy of the Hatch collection.)

Six

EARLY HOMESTEADERS OF TWENTYNINE PALMS

Water was essential for a successful desert homestead. The first 160-acre homesteads were located where there was water not far beneath the surface, and eventually wells were dug, some by hand. Early homesteaders could get their water free from the oasis, or from the Smith Ranch and Bagley's store at the Plaza, but this meant hauling water in whatever containers were available. Early well diggers included Charles Taylor, seen here in 1935. (Courtesy of Pat Rimmington.)

Charles Taylor proudly shows off his well pump in 1935. Taylor was a World War I veteran who filed on a homestead in Twentynine Palms in 1929 and proved up on his land in 1931 with his wife and three children. He drilled water wells for numerous early homesteaders. (Courtesy of Pat Rimmington.)

William "Bill" Smith and his son Raymond, the first homesteader child born in Twentynine Palms, are seen here in 1931. Smith first arrived in 1923 and returned in 1926 to homestead Smith Ranch along Adobe Road. According to pioneer Helen Bagley, he arrived in an old truck with $1.34 in cash and a broken arm. He was a rancher, dairyman, trucker, and well digger. He married Thelma Mead, the daughter of fellow homesteaders, in 1930.

In the mid-1920s, Bill Smith and his brother Harry drilled a well at Smith Ranch that pumped 500 gallons per minute and created a small lake. Unfortunately for them, Jim Byler's car became mired in it. Smith Ranch had the first reliable source of water, which was freely shared with homesteaders like Byler. Smith also drilled wells for Frank Bagley at what became the Plaza and for the 29 Palms Inn in 1928.

"There were lots of burros roaming the desert," reads the caption on this Smith Ranch photograph featuring, from left to right, Blanche Furniss, Al Northey, Fred Furniss, Doc Foley, and Bill Smith's truck. Many of the burros were descendents of those released by early prospectors. The burros were often caught by the homesteaders and ridden by their children, sometimes to school.

A handmade ladder at the Smith Ranch reached to the second floor where the Smiths ran the projector for their patio theater, the first movie theater in Twentynine Palms. William Underhill would later lease space at the ranch and construct a large indoor theater and auditorium. Smith Ranch also had an icehouse, ice cream parlor, and grocery and today operates one of the last drive-in movie theaters in Southern California.

The Smith family, from left to right, Del Dee, Nona, Gayle, Raymond, parents Thelma and Bill Smith, and youngsters Dessie and David, are seen about 1946–1947. All the children helped with chores around the ranch. Raymond delivered water, David was movie projectionist, and the girls helped their mother in the ice cream parlor, snack bar, and grocery store.

William and Elizabeth Campbell's homestead cabin in the mid-1920s featured a bed, kitchen cabinets made of boxes, a card table for dining, camp chairs, kerosene lamps, and a cook stove on the porch. After months of camping at the oasis and living in a tent on their homestead property, the Campbells cherished their first four walls and a roof. (Photograph by Elizabeth Campbell.)

Collected rocks and materials hauled from Pasadena became this large stone house at Campbell Ranch in the mid-1930s, built adjacent to the homestead cabin (right). It was the most elegant home in Twentynine Palms, the site of many teas and social events, and is now the Roughley Manor. This 1945 photograph was taken when Elizabeth Campbell put the house up for sale following William's tragic death in 1944.

Cabins on the grounds of American Legion Desert Outpost 334 served as temporary lodging for veterans, schoolteachers, and other new arrivals in the early days of Twentynine Palms. The grounds also had the first public swimming pool in the area, built entirely by community volunteers in 1929, and the Legion Café was used for high school classes from 1934 to 1937. The site is now part of Luckie Park. (Courtesy of Jim Bagley.)

The first court trial in Twentynine Palms was held at the Legion Café in 1930–1931. The jury acquitted the defendants, who were accused of shooting a deer out of season. Twentynine Palms Judicial District was formed in February 1930 when a petition with 65 signatures was approved. Sam Bailey was appointed justice of the peace with Guy Mattox appointed constable. Later that year, Louis Jacobs was elected justice of the peace and Gus Seely constable.

Dr. James B. Luckie, a Pasadena physician, sent World War I veterans afflicted with respiratory ailments to live and homestead in the dry climate of Twentynine Palms. He later donated 40 acres of land to the American Legion Desert Outpost 334, which became part of Luckie Park, dedicated in his honor shortly before his death in 1965. He is regarded as the "Father of Twentynine Palms." (Courtesy of Susan Luckie Reilly.)

Luckie Park was dedicated on July 4, 1965. At the dedication were, from left to right, William Underhill, who gave the history of American Legionnaires of Twentynine Palms; Frank Bagley, legionnaire; Susan Luckie Moore, daughter of Dr. Luckie; Dr. James B. Luckie; John Bagley, legionnaire; Dale Vaughn, commander of Post 334; Chester Ellis, chamber of commerce president; Rev. LeLand Kuns, who made the dedication; and William Procter, recreation district superintendent.

Walter E. Ketcham named his desert homestead Rancho Dipodomys for the little kangaroo rats that frequented the area. An article on Ketcham and his furry friends was published in the October 1940 issue of *National Geographic*, bringing much recognition to Twentynine Palms. The writer and animal lover was also the second local member, along with pioneer Helen Bagley, to serve on the original Morongo District school board.

"Drop the cup and the air is filled with bouncing balls of fur," Walter Ketcham said of his daily dipodomys feeding ritual. Ketcham protected the dipodomys on his homestead and fed them well. Parents would often bring their children to the ranch, located off Amboy Road in Twentynine Palms, to feed and play with the shy little kangaroo rats.

William B. "Bill" Hatch Jr.'s cabin in Twentynine Palms had been used in the Athletics Village in Los Angeles during the 1932 Olympics. It consisted of two rooms separated by a bathroom. Hatch had it disassembled and moved to his 160-acre homestead in Twentynine Palms, which was on a hill with a 360-degree view of open desert. (Photograph by Bill Hatch.)

A sand road near Twentynine Palms Oasis accommodates Bill Hatch's Model A Ford. Rutted roads ruled in the 1930s and were subject to frequent flash floods. The road from Highway 99 up the Morongo grade was little more than two tracks in the sand, dodging boulders and creosote with no room for two cars to pass. Trucks had the right-of-way, and motorists had to pull off to the side.

A new, 3,000-gallon water tank and windmill are being installed at the Hatch homestead on Utah Trail in this 1936 photograph. Called the "30th Palm," the property contained a house, a well, and a light plant on five acres, which had been acquired by Bill Hatch from Gordon Bains for $1,000 in the 1930s. At the time, the house had one of the only indoor bathtubs in Twentynine Palms. (Photograph by Bill Hatch.)

Ada Hatch, seen in her square-dance costume, was a member of Scripps College's first graduating class in 1931 and obtained a master's degree in Child Development from Columbia University. Ada first came to the desert in 1936 and returned in 1937 as the wife of Bill Hatch. She later helped establish Little Church of the Desert preschool and the Friends of Copper Mountain College, which built a community college in the area.

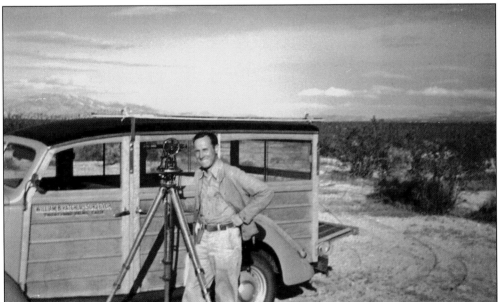

Bill Hatch surveys tract 2654 in April 1941. A California Institute of Technology graduate, he came to Twentynine Palms in 1932 and maintained the light plant at 29 Palms Inn. He remained in the desert and became a leading citizen, using his surveying skills to layout the cemetery, the town, and the homesteads, and later helped create the flood-control channel that diverted flash floods from raging through the center of town. (Photograph by Ada Hatch.)

A new Chevrolet was a novelty in the desert in 1936, especially for the Malone children. Pictured are, from left to right, Donald, Clare, and Peter. Edward Malone, a World War I veteran with war-related respiratory disabilities, discovered Twentynine Palms in 1929 after learning of the healthful environment from fellow veterans in Pasadena. He and his wife, Kathryn, homesteaded 160 acres on Amboy Road, where Walter Berg built them a concrete block house. Donald became an art instructor at Twentynine Palms High School for 28 years.

Frank and Mildred DeMent homesteaded 160 acres in 1925 at the northwest corner of Mesquite Springs Road and Indian Trail, where they grew fruits such as oranges, grapefruit, grapes, peaches, and dates, and a variety of vegetables. They had a dozen dairy cows, numerous chickens and turkeys, and a team of horses to plow their alfalfa field.

The Stubbs brothers were stockbrokers in Chicago when the market crashed, and they moved to Twentynine Palms in 1930. William C. "Bill" and Elisha G. "Lish" Stubbs learned to build with adobe bricks while constructing their homestead. Soon they were constructing other adobe homes and businesses and eventually had 50 employees. Lish, seen here with dog Snubber in 1932, later opened Stubbs Paint Pot on Adobe Road, and Bill had a clothing store and a shoe store at the Plaza.

The first room of the Stubbs brothers' adobe had a humble interior in October 1932. The southwest corner of the kitchen shows a temporarily installed heavy door, which would eventually be used as the front door. The bookshelves were made of apple boxes painted black.

Bill and Lish Stubbs homesteaded 160 acres eight miles northwest of the Plaza in Twentynine Palms in 1930. Working with Charles Taylor and his wife, they drilled a well, striking good water at 125 feet, and experimented with making bricks from adobe hauled from Mesquite Dry Lake. Lumber was obtained from a dismantled telephone building, and they salvaged doors and windows from a wrecking yard in Redlands. The house was built one room at a time.

Lida and Hassell Donnell homesteaded in Twentynine Palms in 1925. Because of her husband's southern hospitality and their nonpaying guests, Lida decided to open a hotel. Donnell Desert Hotel opened in 1928, later called the Mission Inn and photographed here in 1938. The hotel and 29 Palms Inn were the only places to stay at that time. Winter rates in 1939 were single $5 and up, double $8 and up, breakfast 50¢, lunch 75¢, and dinner $1.

The Adobe Hotel on Two Mile Road is pictured in 1938. Jack McClane and Edward White built the 12-room hotel in 1935 on their 320-acre hill overlooking Twentynine Palms. In 1937, the exclusive resort and 10 acres were sold to Albert Miller and Col. H. L. Watson. With a swimming pool, a large dining room, and a well-stocked bar, it hosted social gatherings and was a showplace in the community.

The inside of the Adobe Hotel in 1938 was cozy and comfortable with a fireplace to gather around on cold winter evenings. Reading; a game of cards, bridge, or Michigan (a popular game in the 1930s); or just some good conversation were after-dinner activities. It was a place to get away from it all.

The Circle C Motel, known today as the Circle C Lodge, was built in the late 1940s or early 1950s. A swimming pool was a welcome amenity for weary desert travelers in those days, and Circle C was one of several new motels that accommodated the tourists attracted to Twentynine Palms for its healthful climate, its proximity to what is now Joshua Tree National Park, and its availability of homestead land.

Col. E. B. Moore was an early realtor and promoter of five-acre, "jackrabbit" homesteads. The desert was opened to five-acre homesteads by the 1938 Small Claims Act, which made available former Bureau of Land Management (BLM) land throughout the Mojave Desert, although the rush did not start until the 1950s. Moore was said to have helped some 10,000 people file on the homesteads for as little as $10 an acre. (Courtesy of Joan Jackson.)

Seven

BAGLEY STORE AND THE PLAZA

The early business district of Twentynine Palms in 1927 was the combination Bagley home and store in what would become known as the Plaza. This converted 18-by-18-foot garage was the family home at night and a general store during the day, after the double bed was rolled outside to make room for visitors and potential customers. An old 10-by-14-foot tent was later obtained, which served as the family sleeping quarters until a permanent house could be built.

A two-car garage on a cement slab was both the home and store of Frank and Helen Bagley and their three boys—John, six; Alan, three; and Denny, four months—when they came to Twentynine Palms during Thanksgiving 1927. Four 5-foot shelves were built to hold the groceries, which had to be purchased in Banning 60 miles away. The gas pump provided extra income from the occasional traveler. (Courtesy of Jim Bagley.)

Enterprising businessman Frank Bagley soon made additions to his garage home and store. An extra building (right) eventually became the post office, where he served as postmaster from 1930 to 1937. Bagley tirelessly helped arriving homesteaders find their property, grubstaked many a miner, and carried struggling settlers on his books at the store. He was also active in the Lions Club, the American Legion, and Little Church of the Desert. (Courtesy of Jim Bagley.)

Playing in front of Bagley's combination home and store in 1928 from left to right are Alan Bagley, Marge and Bob Phillips, John Bagley, and toddler Denny Bagley. Helen Bagley (far right) helped run the store and pump gas while taking care of her children. She grew to love the desert. Her book *Sand in My Shoe*, published in 1978, recounts the early days of the homesteaders of Twentynine Palms.

The blackboard at the Bagley store served as a newspaper in the early 1930s. The first printed news was the *Outpost*, published by the American Legion in 1932. The Bagley store also housed a small shelf of books, which became a library. Helen Bagley served as San Bernardino County branch librarian from 1930 to 1940, following Frances Roberts who ran the first library at Gold Park Hotel. Helen also served on the school board from 1928 to 1938.

Denny Bagley sits on the hood of an old truck at the Plaza with his companion, the family dog Skippy, on the fender. Skippy was known all over town and often caught rides in neighbors' cars. (Courtesy of Jim Bagley.)

The Tom Mix Straight Shooters Club was an offshoot of the radio program sponsored by Ralston Purina that was listened to by early homesteaders' children lucky enough to have a radio. Many premiums were offered, including badges, guns, books, lariats, and bandanas. In this 1934 photograph are club members, from left to right, Bruce Curry, Lester Krushat, Billy Barnett, Harold Hockett, Alan Bagley, Buddy Whitehead, Eugene Curry on burro, Lloyd Godwin, and Bobby Graham.

Tom Martin's garage at the Plaza opened in 1930 next to Bagley's store (far right). The Martins first came to Twentynine Palms in 1928. After a brief return to Illinois in 1934 for two years, they settled in Twentynine Palms permanently to raise their three sons, Derald, Troy, and Chuck. Martin also drove and maintained the local school bus.

The entire business community in 1932 at the Plaza in Twentynine Palms is shown in this photograph taken at Graham's Lunch Room. Pictured from left to right are Tom Martin, Art Krushat, Helen Bagley, Imogene Aaron, Hilda Graham, Jimmy Graham, and Frank Bagley. The Grahams later built their new and much larger Graham's Café in the Plaza in 1937.

When plumber Ed Duquette put a "City Hall" sign on the tank house at the Plaza as a joke and someone sent a photograph to Ripley's *Believe It Or Not*, "the smallest city hall in the world" became internationally known. "City Hall," seen here in 1933, was actually a water tower owned by the Bagleys and used by homesteaders as a source of free water, showers, and a barbershop with Johnny Kee officiating. (Photograph by Bill Hatch.)

The first elected justice of the peace, Louis Jacobs (left), who served from 1930 to 1935, performed the first wedding at "City Hall." Nell and Walt Godwin flank the newlyweds, Helen Jean Smart and Harry Godwin, on December 31, 1933. Jacobs, a mining engineer, came to the area around 1919. He was tract manager for Pinto Basin Land Company in the mid-1920s, a mining reporter for the *Outpost*, and president of the newly formed chamber of commerce.

Before electricity and refrigeration, the availability of ice was a big deal for desert homesteaders. The first ice plant in Twentynine Palms was the Desert Ice and Storage Company located at the Plaza. Owned by Ted Holderman and completed in 1934, it had the capacity of producing two tons of ice a day. The adobe brick building, constructed by the Stubbs brothers, eventually became the Twentynine Palms Historical Society's first museum (1982–1983). It was torn down after being damaged in the Landers earthquake of 1992. Pictured above is the first block of locally made ice being delivered to Graham's Lunch Room in 1934. From left to right are James Graham, Eddie Kull, Frank Bagley, Hilda Graham, Denny Bagley, and Ted Holderman. The Smith Ranch icehouse and ice cream parlor pictured below was built about 1935. (Courtesy of Pat Graham Burfield and Pat Rimmington.)

The new Bagley Market at the Plaza opened January 2, 1937. Nearly 1,000 people attended a preview party on November 28, 1936. They danced to music of a trio that included the Bagley's eldest son John on steel guitar and Les Cross on banjo. It was the largest crowd ever assembled in Twentynine Palms at that point in time. Also in this 1938 photograph is the new Graham's Café (left). (Photograph by Harlow Jones.)

The Plaza in Twentynine Palms was busy in 1939. The Plaza area was laid out in 1936 as a shopping center, which was not a common idea at the time. It had a wide parking area and grouped stores with a village atmosphere. Philip Zimmers Sr. was the architect of many of the buildings. (Photograph by Harlow Jones.)

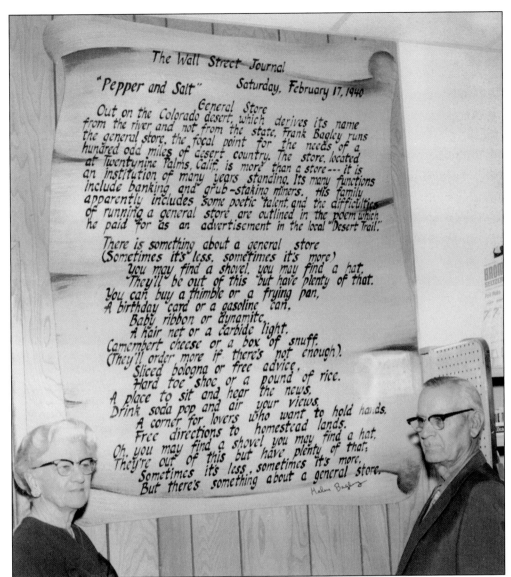

The Wall Street Journal

"Pepper and Salt"   Saturday, February 17, 1940

General Store

Out on the Colorado desert, which derives its name from the river and not from the state, Frank Bagley runs the general store, the focal point for the needs of a hundred odd miles of desert country. The store, located at Twentynine Palms, Calif. is more than a store --- it is an institution of many years standing. Its many functions include banking and grub-staking miners. His family apparently includes some poetic talent and the difficulties of running a general store are outlined in the poem which he paid for as an advertisement in the local "Desert Trail."

There is something about a general store
(Sometimes it's less, sometimes it's more.)
    You may find a shovel, you may find a hat,
    They'll be out of this but have plenty of that.
You can buy a thimble or a frying pan,
A birthday card or a gasoline can.
    Baby ribbon or dynamite,
    A hair net or a carbide light.
Camembert cheese or a box of snuff.
(They'll order more if there's not enough.)
    Sliced bologna or free advice,
    Hard toe shoe or a pound of rice.
A place to sit and hear the news,
Drink soda pop and air your views.
    A corner for lovers who want to hold hands.
    Free directions to homestead lands.
Oh, you may find a shovel you may find a hat.
They're out of this but have plenty of that.
    Sometimes it's less, sometimes it's more.
    But there's something about a general store.

                                            Helen Bagley

Another proud moment for the growing desert community of Twentynine Palms happened when Helen Bagley's poem "Salt and Pepper" appeared in the *Wall Street Journal* on February 17, 1940. Frank and Helen are seen here in their later years with a reproduction of the poem mounted on the wall of Bagley's Market. (Courtesy of Jim Bagley.)

During World War II, the rationing line in front of Bagley's Market at the Plaza around 1942 was especially long on Bacon Day, but the wait was definitely worthwhile for those lucky enough to have a coupon and to get some before the supply was exhausted.

This gas rationing card was issued January 17, 1945, to L. L. Tower for a three-month period. Lilly L. Tower was the wife of Herbert Tower, who homesteaded east of town in 1934. Herb worked for many years at Bagley's Market at the Plaza. Their daughter, Dona, still lives at the old homestead on Amboy Road in the Wonder Valley area of Twentynine Palms.

Judge Dave Poste operated the first telephone switchboard in his adobe home at the Plaza and contracted with California Water and Telephone Company in 1936 with seven subscribers. Poste and his wife, Anna, came in 1923 to operate the Virginia Dale Mine. During the Depression, they moved into town. Seen here in 1949, Poste served as justice of the peace for the Twentynine Palms Judicial District from 1935 until his retirement in 1951. (Courtesy of Art Kidwell.)

Blanche Loomis Ellis was hired by Judge Poste to operate the switchboard in 1948. She provided personal service for callers, often tracking people around town to relay messages. Blanche arrived in 1946 with son Gene to manage Las Casitas Motel at the Plaza, owned by her sister Grace. She was an avid horsewoman and was credited with teaching actress Esther Williams to ride. Blanche eventually married local bachelor Chet Ellis, whom she met over the phone.

Doc McKittrick, known as "Radio Doc," took over, from left to right, Bagley's first store, the old post office building, and Graham's Lunch Room in 1939 and started a business that offered electrical appliance sales and service and as he advertised, "everything in radio."

What looks like an attempted jailbreak at the original County of San Bernardino Jail in Twentynine Palms was actually the result of a runaway gas tanker when its air brakes failed on May 16, 1949. The small jail in the Plaza was only used to hold male prisoners until they could be transported to San Bernardino or attend one of the few trials that were held at the American Legion Hall at what is now Luckie Park. (Photograph by Ted Richardson.)

Eight

Four Corners Business Development

An aerial view of the Four Corners area of Twentynine Palms in 1940–1941 shows the slowly growing downtown business district, which began to compete with early commerce in the Plaza to the north. Four Corners was named for the intersection of north-south Adobe Road and east-west One Mile Road, the main route into town, which became Highway 62 and later Twentynine Palms Highway. (Photograph by Harlow Jones.)

The desert highway in 1933 was just two ruts in the sand. Since the need for roads was paramount to the development of the area, Twentynine Palms Road and Improvement Association was formed in 1927 with Bill Campbell as chairman and treasurer, and Bill Bixby, a graduate of the California Institute of Technology, who was in charge of surveying. (Photograph by Bill Hatch.)

A meeting was held at 29 Palms Inn on February 5, 1932, to discuss placement of new roads in Twentynine Palms. Existing main roads were One Mile (the present Highway 62), Two Mile, and Three Mile, the present Amboy Road. Road construction was a large community effort. The able-bodied graded and cleared brush, while others contributed money. The women made and delivered lunches for the men. (Photograph by Bill Hatch.)

The 29 Palms Village real estate office of Hamilton Sales Corporation sat on the southeast corner of Four Corners in 1936. The 29 Palms Village development was located in an area close to the Oasis of Mara. Hamilton also developed Adobe Acres on a hillside south of the Plaza, which they advertised as the "high spot of the desert."

Leonard Wikoff (left), seen here with Tom Martin in 1940, installed the first generator, a 25-horsepower Fairbanks-Morse diesel generator for electrical power at Four Corners in 1937 with 14 consumers. It became Wikoff Electric Light and Power. Years would pass before power was available throughout the community. When the business was sold in 1944 to California Electric Power Company, it had 50 miles of pole lines, 75 transformers, and some 600 customers. (Courtesy of Jim Bagley.)

The Desert Estates development office (right) for Pacific Coast Land Company sold tracts in the Smoketree area of Twentynine Palms, west of Donnell Hill, advertised as "On the Miracle Mile," in 1936. Schneider-Bunker Company handled sales, and Chester R. Bunker, former city editor of the *Los Angeles Herald,* was tract manager. Lots were listed at $150 and up, and the Stubbs brothers constructed the adobe homes. This building later became Dean's Coffee Shop.

Warner's Grill at Four Corners in 1938 sat next to the Southwest Subdividers, Limited, tower (right), which promoted their development of the 29 Palms Townsite.

Developer Ole Hanson's office (right) is seen at Four Corners in 1938. Hanson developed the area's pioneer subdivision southeast of Four Corners in 1936, named Desert Homes but called the "Hanson Tract" by locals to this day. Hanson was a former mayor of Seattle and founder and developer of San Clemente before coming to Twentynine Palms. Hanson was attracted by the healthy climate and low cost of land. Next door is the E. H. Nicholes brokerage office.

Union Oil Station North Gate Service and market were at Four Corners in 1938. Clovis and Mary Benito moved the business in 1937 from its old location at the corner of Sullivan and Adobe when the main highway was rerouted over Donnell Hill, making Sullivan Road secondary. The station remained in this spot until the 1990s. It is now the site of a Denny's Restaurant.

Joshua Tree Inn Café, now the Virginian, was a well-regarded eatery in the 1930s. Its addition, called "The Barn," was popular for banquets and Saturday night dances. Major and Helen Huber sold their interest in 1943 to Bob Paylor, coordinator for commissaries at Twentynine Palms Air Academy. Frances Duffy owned the beauty shop next door, and the Gilpin's Plumbing adobe building (far right) is now How How Chinese Restaurant.

This is the Sunkist Garage in downtown Twentynine Palms as it appeared in 1938. Ernest Robinson opened the first new car dealership in town at this location in 1939, selling Dodge and Plymouth vehicles. The building is now Hi-Desert Tire.

Dean's Coffee Shop at Four Corners in 1948–1949 was a favorite gathering place for locals. In 1950, it was bought by Charlie Matherly, former head of maintenance at Twentynine Palms Air Academy's glider school during World War II. Often open 24 hours, it became a pick-up point for passengers en route to Las Vegas. It is now the site of Bank of America ATMs. (Photograph by Eddie Adams.)

The first drugstore, called 29 Palms Drug Company, was located one block east of Four Corners and established by Jesse White in February 1936. Carl Pomeroy was pharmacist. It was put up by Southwest Subdividers, Limited, for the new 29 Palms Townsite and was noted for its soda fountain, the first one in town. The drugstore was also the scene of the first robbery in January 1937.

Barbara Page's Desert Gift Shop was built by Walter Berg in the 1930s. Seen here in 1940, it was later extensively modified in 1954 by realtors Chet and Lois Knee and called The Red Barn. Chet came to Twentynine Palms in 1942 as a tow pilot and instructor at Condor Field. He returned in 1947 and went into real estate with homesteader Bob McCown. Today the building is Red Barn Realty. (Photograph by Harlow Jones.)

Ada Hatch sits in her Model A Ford during a flash flood on the highway in 1938. Her engineer husband, Bill, was appointed flood control commissioner and served for 34 years. He helped to create the flood control channel that ultimately diverted raging waters from the downtown business area. His guidance and leadership were recognized by the San Bernardino County Board of Supervisors in 1973. (Photograph by Bill Hatch.)

This view looking east on the highway shows the downtown area of Twentynine Palms in the early 1940s. Kenney's Drug Store (right) is in its original location on the southeast corner of Tamarisk Avenue and the highway, before the business moved across the street. The building is now Wonder Garden Café. (Photograph by Harlow Jones.)

Joshua Monument National Bank, built in 1948, was the first bank in Twentynine Palms. Prior to its arrival, banking entailed driving some 60 miles to Banning. Honorary mayor Esther Williams presided at its opening. Roscoe Coon, bank vice president and cashier, was later convicted of embezzling funds to play the horses and was sentenced to prison for 20 years. The building later became Security Pacific Bank and is now Edchada's Mexican Restaurant. (Photograph by Burton Frasher.)

Ken Forman's Desert Market Basket opened on the highway in Twentynine Palms in 1950. The building was remodeled by Dawn Benton Sr. in 1963 and became Benton Brothers variety store. After two expansions in 1970 and 1976, it eventually covered the entire block between Yucca Avenue and Tamarisk Avenue. In 2000, the building was remodeled again by Dawn Benton Jr. and Jay McCormick and reopened as Desert Ranch Market, now the Rio Ranch Market.

Dawn Benton Sr., an experienced variety store manager, came to Twentynine Palms in 1959 to buy Beulah Smith's Dime Store. In 1963, he moved across the highway and opened Benton Brothers, named for his partnership with brother Jerry. The store expanded twice, once in 1970 and again in 1976. It was a vital community outlet for housewares, appliances, clothing, and toys until it closed in 1999. His son, Dawn Jr., worked for 25 years in the store and later became mayor.

The Hatch Insurance and Land Surveying building east of the Plaza weathered the big snow of January 1949 when a record 12 to 15 inches of snow fell throughout the town. In the outlying areas, the snow was so deep that Bavarian-born resident Barbara Grether, who had just moved to Twentynine Palms with her family a year earlier, used her skis to bring food to trapped homesteaders.

This aerial view of Twentynine Palms Highway in 1949 was taken east of Four Corners looking west. The Shingle Inn is on the lower right with Four Corners, where Adobe Road intersects the highway, at the center. Barely visible in the distance is the water tank on Donnell Hill in the upper left. (Photograph by Eddie Adams.)

Kenney's Drug Store moved west across Tamarisk to its new highway location in November 1947, where it served the community until closing in November 1995. Edward Kenney took on pharmacist Albert Beller as a partner in 1958, and in 1980, Carol Barrett bought the store when Kenney retired. Arriving with his wife, Margaret, in 1940, Kenney was also a community leader and instrumental in building Blessed Sacrament Church and Hi-Desert Medical Center.

Photographer Ted Richardson and his wife, Mabel, moved to Twentynine Palms in 1949 and opened a photography studio on Adobe Road. Two locations later, he moved into the old Kenney's Drug, pictured in 1955, which is now Wonder Garden Café. Their son Noble worked in the studio and became an accomplished artist with a studio of his own in 1992 in the Benito, later DeWitt, building at Sullivan and Adobe Roads. (Courtesy of Gene Kenney.)

Depicted in the photograph, the building complex in the lower left on south Adobe Road is the Twentynine Palms fire station and living quarters, built in 1944 and pictured in 1948. In the county equipment area at the rear, an old garage was formerly utilized by Joshua Tree National Monument as its headquarters. It was extensively remodeled in 1954 and became the new jail. The building on the right was Petrolie's Italian Restaurant, now the senior center. (Photograph by Harlow Jones.)

El Rancho Dolores Motel opened in 1940 on the highway near Four Corners. It is shown here about 1949–1950 when it was owned and operated by Mr. and Mrs. H. F. Perkins. The motel was advertised as "open all year" with "moderate rates, $4 up." The motel is still part of downtown Twentynine Palms and now is operated by the Ken Patel family. (Photograph by Ted Richardson.)

The Shell station on the northwest corner of Four Corners was owned by Earl Carris in 1938, Burt King in 1942, and Chester "Chet" Ellis in 1951. Chet and his wife, Blanche, also operated the ambulance service, using station employees as drivers during the day while they took responsibility at night. Chet was president of the chamber of commerce from 1964 to 1965, and the couple served as Pioneer Days grand marshals in 1988. (Photograph by the *Desert Trail*.)

Harry and Frances Sabol moved their Sabol's Trading Post from San Bernardino to Twentynine Palms in 1957 and operated the popular business on Raymond Avenue until 1969. Harry was a businessman, an artist, and a supporter of the Twentynine Palms Artists Guild. Frances was a mathematics teacher and active in Camping Women and the Twentynine Palms Historical Society. Together they started the United Methodist Church in Twentynine Palms in 1959.

K-B Mart opened in May 1962 on the highway in the Smoketree area of Twentynine Palms, built by K-B partners Edward Kenney and Albert Beller. Wallace Bradfield was store manager. Beller, a pharmacist who arrived in 1956 from Arizona with his wife, Mary Ann, and their children, became a partner in Kenney's Drug in 1958 and opened the first K-B Liquor and Delicatessen next door. (Courtesy of Margaret Kenney.)

This rendering shows Jimmy Williams's Smoke Tree Supper Club, where diners could enjoy a lobster dinner for $3 and a dry martini for 60¢ in 1951. Formerly the Smoke Tree Broiler, opened in the Smoke Tree Villas area by Phil Albert in January 1938, it was acquired in May by Williams, who booked acts from Los Angeles and Palm Springs, giving Twentynine Palms its first night club. In the mid-1960s, it became the first Josh Lounge.

John and Clara Dobler, owners of Hi-Desert Food Service, moved to Twentynine Palms from Chicago in 1953. Their children, known as the seven Cs, were Christopher, Cynthia, Cassandra, Catherine, Clifford, Conrad, and Corrine. John drove to Riverside daily to bring fresh dairy products to the town. They later expanded to carry beer, wine, soda, fresh fruits, and vegetables. The Dobler family came to Twentynine Palms to find a cure for Clifford's asthma.

John and Clara's son, Conrad Dobler, had a distinguished football career as an offensive lineman. He played college ball at the University of Wyoming and went on to star in professional football with the St. Louis Cardinals, New Orleans Saints, and Buffalo Bills. Fans, coaches, and opposing players called him the "Meanest Man in Pro Football."

Nine

COMMUNITY SERVICES
IN THE DESERT

The one-room schoolhouse in Twentynine Palms was built in 1927 by community volunteers who raised $300 for materials. Located on five acres of land donated by the Campbells, the building measured 20 by 28 feet. The homesteaders built it themselves, since their request for funds had been turned down by the County of San Bernardino superintendent of schools, Ida Collins, who thought Twentynine Palms would never prosper. School opened in November with nine local students plus the two children of a county-provided teacher. (Courtesy of Derald Martin collection.)

The first school in Twentynine Palms was located east of Gold Park Road, now Utah Trail. The teacher, Miss Daniels (right), is seen with a friend in 1923. Classes were held in the building that was formerly a Gold Park Mining Company office. The tent at right was the teacher's living quarters. The school had seven students from the Tucker and Smith families. (Photograph by Maud Russell.)

The Reverend Howard and Della Dudley taught students including the Eaton, Keys, Randolph, McRoberts, Dudley, and Headington children, at the Keys's ranch schoolhouse from 1937 to 1942. The Dudleys had been missionaries in Burma for 33 years. Della, not yet ready for retirement, was hired as a teacher by San Bernardino County and sent to the Desert Queen Ranch. Howard gave the morning invocation and helped Bill Keys around the ranch. (Courtesy of Willis Keys.)

Homesteaders built the one-room schoolhouse for Twentynine Palms in 1927. Seated on the left burro are, from left to right, Danny Junker, Bob Hodgdon, John Bagley, and Oskar Kerby. Iolah Cook is holding the left burro, and Dick Strafford is holding the right one. Seated on the right burro are, from left to right, Jim Kerby, Fred Strafford, and Edwin Cooke.

The schoolhouse added a second room in 1931 due to an overflow of students. Two teachers were employed for the first time in 1931. The second room was designed so it could be used as a community hall, where dances were held on Saturday nights and church groups met on Sundays. The shaded front porch was used at lunch hour and as a stage for graduation exercises. (Courtesy of Alan Bagley.)

The original schoolhouse was given to Twentynine Palms Historical Society for $1 in 1991 by the Morongo Unified School District, with the stipulation that it be moved to a new location within two years. The entire community joined the effort and raised approximately $100,000 for moving and refurbishing the building. The journey of two miles down Utah Trail took place on April 4, 1992, led by a Marine Corps Honor Guard, the Twentynine Palms High School Marching Band, parents, children, dogs, and well-wishers. The historic move was filmed by Huell Howser for his KCET-TV series, *California's Gold*. After the move to its permanent site at 6760 National Park Drive, the building became the "Old Schoolhouse Museum" and historical society office. It sits on a four-acre parcel across the street from 29 Palms Inn and the Oasis of Mara.

The local Parent Teacher Club, seen at a 29 Palms Inn luncheon in 1932, became affiliated with the national Parent Teacher Association in 1933. Early homesteaders placed a high value on education, freely donating their time and resources. Sarah Jessup, an early teacher, remembers parents sending soup bones and vegetables to school so that hot soup could be made for lunch on cold winter days, and the kids carried their own bowls.

Theodore "Ted" and Mary Hayes first lived in an American Legion cabin in what is now Luckie Park when Ted was hired in 1934 as the first high schoolteacher. He taught all the required classes as well as physical education and manual training, while Mary taught music. When Twentynine Palms High School became affiliated with the Victorville District two years later, Ted was named principal. His tenure lasted 35 years.

The 1937, Twentynine Palms High School students posed in front of the Legion Hall, which is now in Luckie Park. From left to right are (first row) John Bagley, Bill Holmes, Bob Phillips, Bill Bobo, Frank George, Bill Krushat, Doug Pomeroy, Norman Punter, and Stan Krushat; (second row) Helen Strickler, Lois Shelton, Marjorie Stonecipher, Helen Roarshack, Jimmy Page, Jack King, Francis Duffy, Odette Roarshack, Janet Benito, Dorothy Deardorff, and Adele Helfend; (third row) Principal Ted Hayes, Ruth Binkley, Miss Van Kirk (half head), Harold Skinner, Lloyd Guelick, Derald Martin, Valerie Hinshaw, June Kerr, and Alan Bobo. The first Twentynine Palms High School building, pictured below in 1937–1938, eventually became the junior high. The adjacent football field was dedicated as Tom Nicoll Memorial Field in the 1970s, with the urging and support of his widow, Mary, in honor of the former vice principal.

The first class of Twentynine Palms High School graduated in 1937 and consisted of five students. Those historic graduates are, from left to right, Adele Helfend, Derald Martin (salutatorian), Valerie Hinshaw, Bill Krushat, and Janet Benito (valedictorian). Classes were held at the leased Legion Café starting in 1934 and a tiny cabin on the Legion grounds in what is now Luckie Park. A baccalaureate was held at the grammar school, today the Old Schoolhouse Museum, and the graduation ceremony was held in the gymnasium of the newly completed high school, which is now the junior high. Principal Ted Hayes began as the sole teacher, teaching all subjects. When the student body grew to 30 students in the second year, another teacher, Miss Van Kirk, was added.

This early church service was held in a settler's cabin built by Howard Burk. From left to right are (first row) the Episcopal minister, prospector Karl Frederic Jenson, Barbara Hicks, Ethelyn Hicks, Mary Tucker, Albert Smith, Georgeina Hicks, Nathan Hicks, Nelson Tucker, and Hugh Tucker; (second row) Allen Hicks, Katherine Tucker, Bernice Tucker, Miss Daniels (schoolteacher), Mrs. George Hicks, Catherine Hicks, George Hicks, and ? Smith. (Photograph by Maud Russell.)

Little Church of the Desert was dedicated on November 6, 1940. Pictured in 1941, it was a community church in which Catholics and Episcopalians held services, and it was the home of the Presbyterian church. Founding pastor was the Reverend C. D. "Cap" Williamson. The Lions Club donated 30 percent of the $4,500 construction cost, and local architect Philip Zimmers Sr. donated his services. William Watkins was the contractor. (Photograph by Harlow Jones.)

The first Catholic church in Twentynine Palms was located at 6461 Cholla Avenue. The converted building was a church from about 1942 to 1948, with the south half being a rectory and the north half serving as the church. Parishioners refurbished the building, built an altar, installed pews, and put up a steeple. Father Rastall worked with the parish volunteers. (Photograph by Harlow Jones.)

Blessed Sacrament Catholic Church and rectory was built in its present home on National Park Drive in 1948 and was officially dedicated on February 12, 1949. An ongoing fund-raising campaign was aided by Harry G. Johansing, who also donated the land. The parish pastor was Fr. Patrick O'Dowd, who received support from parishioners he called the "Three Wise Men," Robert Van Lahr, Edward Kenney, and Robert Lear. Walter Berg was the contractor, and Claude Powell of Palm Springs was the architect.

Setting the cornerstone for Ince Memorial Hospital on November 19, 1947, are, from left to right, Sally Ince, Walter Berg (contractor), Mrs. Thomas H. Ince (Dr. Ince's mother), and Dr. William Ince. Sealed into the cornerstone was a tin box containing a copy of the *Desert Trail*, a picture of Dr. Ince, a 1947 Roosevelt dime, a half pint of Yellowstone whiskey, and several 3¢ stamps commemorating the 50th anniversary of motion pictures in which Thomas H. Ince was a pioneer producer.

Thomas H. Ince Memorial Hospital on Adobe Road opened on June 19, 1948, as the first hospital in the Morongo Basin. The Inces ran the facility until it was purchased by the newly formed Hospital District in April 1962. In 1963, with the passing of a $185,000 ballot initiative, it became Twentynine Palms Community Hospital. In 1977, it became Hi-Desert Servicemen's Center, now Faith in The Word Christian Center.

Dr. Edward Lincoln Smith and his wife, Betty Ann, are seen as Pioneer Days grand marshals in 1977. In 1940, Smith, a Yale and Harvard Medical School graduate, joined the Navy Medical Corps, serving with the marines on Guadalcanal during World War II. Following the war, he filled the need for a doctor in Twentynine Palms. He practiced for 33 years, delivering around 1,500 babies. (Photograph by Art Kidwell.)

Jack Cones, the legendary "Flying Constable," homesteaded in Twentynine Palms in 1929. Appointed constable in 1932 and elected five times, he used his Piper J-3 Cub airplane to patrol the 2,800-square-mile jurisdiction and built a private airstrip near his home, which was in town. Cones was an active volunteer who helped build roads and drove the community ambulance. He died in February 1960 when his airplane crashed shortly after takeoff from Yucca Valley airport.

Johnnie Hastie's original 29 Palms Stage rode in the Pioneer Days Parade in 1957. It was a 12-passenger bus body mounted on a 1928 Chevrolet chassis. The inaugural service to Banning, 60 miles away, began on November 15, 1938, and the bus contained a wood-burning stove for passenger comfort on cold days. He charged 10¢ for customer orders like produce, flowers, medicine, poultry, clothes, and thread, and he even did their banking.

Johnnie Hastie's second bus was a 1935 Dodge. The fare to Banning was $1.50. Hastie also ran a taxi service in Twentynine Palms and charged 5¢ for going anywhere in town. He sold the business to Ardella Cook in 1973 who renamed it Desert Stage Lines.

The first and only airmail dispatched from Twentynine Palms occurred on May 19, 1938. The mail was picked up from postmaster Benjamin H. Steeg by pony mail carriers and delivered to pilot Roger Crawford at Mesquite Dry Lake. Schools were dismissed early, and school buses joined a parade of cars to the airstrip. Some 500 people witnessed the event, sponsored by the Lions Club, which commemorated the 20th anniversary of U.S. Air Mail service.

Twentynine Palms Airport was originally an emergency landing field for glider operations at the army's Condor Field during World War II. In 1957, the federal government leased it to Twentynine Palms Airport, Inc., a nonprofit organization formed by local businessmen. During the 1970s, the County of San Bernardino acquired the airport. Pictured in 1974, the airport is still home to private airplanes and Twentynine Palms Soaring Club. (Photograph by Harold O. Weight.)

William J. "Bill" Underhill published the area's first weekly newspaper in 1935, called the *Desert Trail*, named for the long dirt highway he traversed many times since homesteading in Twentynine Palms in 1928. He is seen here at his newly acquired linotype machine in 1937 in the newspaper's first building after moving the business from his homestead. A World War I veteran, he learned the printing trade with on-the-job training at several newspapers, including *Pasadena Star News*.

The first Desert Trail building in Twentynine Palms was built at 5770 Adobe Road in 1937. Designed and constructed by Allen Balch with local material and labor, it was the first business building in the new Adobe Acres subdivision. With no electricity available, publisher Bill Underhill used a kerosene-powered generator and later a single-cylinder diesel engine. In 1938, power lines from Wikoff's plant at Four Corners finally reached the area. (Photograph by Bill Hatch.)

At the *Pasadena Star News*, Bill Underhill met Prudence "Prudie" Mason, seen here in 1940, when he used to visit her boss. When he married Prudie in 1941, she became his associate editor–publisher of the *Desert Trail*. Together they also operated Bill's indoor movie theater and roller-skating rink at Smith's Ranch. In 1945, they built a modern theater at the Plaza, followed in 1952 by the Starlite Drive-in Theater and Starlite Rollerink on Gorgonio Drive.

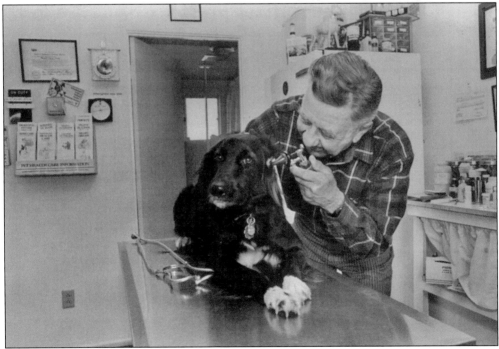

Walter B. "Doc" Crowl, the area's first veterinarian, opened High Desert Animal Hospital in 1954. Having the only X-ray machine around, he was often asked to scan broken bones of local residents in addition to their pets. His wife, Jean, a well-known local artist, recounted the adventures of their small town veterinary practice in her chapbook *Tails from Pill Hill*, written in 1992. (Courtesy of Paul Crowl.)

Twentynine Palms Air Academy hosted a United Service Organization (USO) visit in 1943 at Condor Field, where the U.S. Army opened a glider school in early 1942. During its first 15 months of operation, it trained 1,600 glider pilots, later changing to powered pilot training until closing in April 1944. The U.S. Navy then operated the base as Twentynine Palms Naval Auxiliary Air Station until the end of World War II. (Postcard by Harlow Jones.)

In 1952, Lt. Col. Frederick H. Scantling brought a detachment of two-dozen marines from Camp Pendleton to the old U.S. Army glider base at Condor Field to oversee the building of the Marine Corps Training Center. A civilian construction firm built the new base, supervised by Naval Lt. Comdr. John P. Mapes. Today the 932-square-mile base is the Marine Air Ground Task Force Training Command, Marine Corps Air Ground Combat Center, and the premier live-fire training facility in the world. (Courtesy of Col. Verle E. Ludwig, USMC Ret.)

Ten

Desert Social Life, Art, and Entertainment

A highlight of the social life in Twentynine Palms is the annual Pioneer Days Celebration, which began in May 1936 and continues to this day, held now in October of each year. Pictured in this 1951 parade are, from left to right, Ralph Dunn, Philip H. Zimmers, Nancy Newbranch, Blanche Ellis, Ellen Baskerville, unidentified, Lois Baskerville, and Beth Abell.

Mesquite Dry Lake, a massive, dry lake bed, hosted some of the more unusual desert events during the early Pioneer Day celebrations. This May 1938 photograph captures the starting line for a jalopy race sponsored by the Rod Knockers' Club, a popular event that was said to have drawn as many as 1,000 people. (Photograph by Bill Hatch.)

Land yachting on Mesquite Dry Lake around 1938 was another inventive desert activity in the early days of Twentynine Palms. (Courtesy of the Hatch collection.)

"Pac-a-Pan" Curt Bush and his mule-drawn covered wagon pulled out of Twentynine Palms on March 25, 1940, embarking on a 400-mile trek through the Southland to publicize the fourth annual Pioneer Day Festival and first Desert Rat Convention. The chamber of commerce gave Curt $100 to feed him and the mules for the five-week journey, and he sold pots and pans for extra money. Local artist Roy M. Ropp painted the Oasis of Mara on the wagon's backdrop with the banner "29 Palms Pioneer Day Celebration. All year desert resort—elevation 2,100–5,500—come out and enjoy yourself." The side signs read, "I'm headin' for the Desert Rat Convention—29 Palms, May 4–5." The promotion was successful. Soon investors began to build more housing and motels for increasing numbers of residents and visitors to the area. (Courtesy of Margaret Kenney and Robert Van Lahr.)

The Oasis of Mara hosted early Pioneer Day activities, including this 1940 rodeo event. Locals could enjoy barbecue, archery shoots, equestrian programs, gold panning demonstrations, school concerts, and an old-time "49-er" dance. (Photograph by Harlow Jones.)

Early homesteaders always dressed up for the Pioneer Day Parade. Seen in this 1940 photograph are, from left to right, newlyweds Jim and Elise Dumas Poste, Lida Donnell of Donnell Hotel, and Anna Poste, wife of Judge David Poste and the first known artist in the early days of Twentynine Palms.

A traditional Pioneer Day event is the Little Miss and Master Contest. Contestants pictured in 1947 are, from left to right, Sue Ince, Barbara Dunn, Bob Dunn, Ann Underhill, Sandy Ince, and Stephanie Ince. (Photograph by Eddie Adams.)

Smith Ranch was a favorite social spot in the early years of Twentynine Palms, providing an ice cream parlor, movies, and Saturday night dances. This Pioneer Day Parade float in 1949 includes Marilyn Fernald (left), Nona Smith (right foreground), Roger Jansen, Marie and Herman Fernald, Lee and Hazel Flowers, and Del Dee Smith. (Courtesy of the Smith family.)

Early desert residents could be easily entertained with a fiddle, a guitar, a storyteller, or a homegrown skit. As the community grew, so did stage productions by Twentynine Palms Little Theatre and performance groups like this one in the early 1950s, which included guitarist John Hilton (second from left), guitarist John Bagley (fifth from left), and Blanche Loomis Ellis (second row, third from left.)

The Hometowners social club held a notable Halloween party at the 29 Palms Inn on October 30, 1958, with many prominent citizens and business owners decked out in costume. The inn has been a popular meeting place and site for social gatherings since the late 1920s.

An Easter parade hat contest in the late 1940s featured three prominent women of Twentynine Palms; from left to right are Joan Watkins of M. G. "Watty" Watkins Realty, Margaret Kenney of Kenney's Drug, and Claire Van Lahr of the 29 Palms Inn.

Actress Esther Williams mounted up with the Twentynine Palms Saddle Club for this 1948 outing at Flying W Stables where she first learned to ride. Needing equestrian skills for a movie role, she asked local horsewoman Blanche Loomis Ellis to give her a crash course in horseback riding. Williams often visited her uncle, plumber Ed Gilpin, and her brother Dave Williams, who had moved to the desert for his asthma in 1943.

On March 7, 1948, actress Esther Williams was proclaimed honorary mayor of Twentynine Palms by chamber of commerce president M. G. "Watty" Watkins in a ceremony at the oasis. The day's events included breakfast at Flying W Café, an American Legion barbecue, a fashion show at the Condor Field swimming pool, a reception at the Leonard Wikoff home, dinner at El Adobe Hotel, and an inaugural ball hosted by the Junior Women's Club. (Photograph by Eddie Adams.)

Hollywood movie composer Allie Wrubel was celebrated after winning the 1948 Academy Award for his song "Zip-A-Dee-Doo-Dah," written with lyricist Ray Gilbert for the Walt Disney movie *Song of the South*. Wrubel and his wife, Wanda, owned the Flying W Stables and Café and lived in the only mansion in Twentynine Palms, the former Campbell Ranch, now Roughley Manor, where friends could gather for moonlight rides and rousing parties. (Photograph by Eddie Adams.)

"The Lady from 29 Palms," words and music by resident Allie Wrubel, was published by Martin Music in Hollywood in 1947, introduced by Tony Martin, and recorded by Frank Sinatra and the Andrews Sisters. Wrubel composed for film musicals at Warner Brothers from 1934 through 1946, then signed with Walt Disney Studios. Besides the 1948 Oscar-winning "Zip-A-Dee-Doo-Dah," the composer's catalog of songs ranged from "Gone With The Wind" to "At The Flying W."

Allie Wrubel and Dorothy Partridge sit at the piano where he reportedly composed "The Lady From 29 Palms." Wrubel often entertained musicians and celebrities, such as Johnny Mercer, Jimmy Van Heusen, and Jimmy Durante at his desert home. He purchased the Campbell Ranch in 1946, an 11-room house on 400 acres that included the Flying W Stables. He lived in Twentynine Palms for two decades. (Courtesy of Celeste Gage.)

The first outdoor movies were shown at the patio theater at Smith Ranch. The projector was on the second floor above the ice cream parlor after 1940. Bill and Thelma Smith and Iona Mead are pictured in the theater seating area arranged on their dirt floor patio. Today Smith's Ranch Drive-In in Twentynine Palms has one of the last drive-in movie theaters in Southern California. (Courtesy of the Smith family.)

The Underhills built the first modern movie house in the Morongo Basin, with a neon sign reading "29 Palms Theatre." Grand opening night was held November 10, 1945, and featured *Johnny Angel* starring George Raft. Located at the corner of Adobe Road and Two Mile Road, it had 400 upholstered seats, loges, a glassed-in lobby, and a flagstone front patio. The building also hosted community events and Twentynine Palms Little Theatre plays on the stage.

Isadore Vermette (right) built the first motor home in Twentynine Palms from a converted 1947 Plymouth. Vermette moved from Connecticut in 1941 when the doctors sent him to a dry climate for his asthma. He and Agnes raised six children—Norman, Richard, Jeannette, Gloria, Rita, and Susan—in their home on Utah Trail. He owned the Utah Trail Garage and often performed mechanical work at no charge for local churches and the school district. (Courtesy of the Vermette family.)

The Bowladium has provided nearly six decades of entertainment for Twentynine Palms residents, like "Radio Doc" McKittrick seen here in the 1950s. Jack and Dorothy Lynn began construction in 1949, and it opened in October 1950. George Mintz bought the business in July 1973. Today it still features a bar, originally called the Persian Room; a coffee shop; and open and league bowling. (Courtesy of the McKittrick family.)

Cleaning up the Twentynine Palms Golf Course after a sandstorm in 1966, these resident golfers are seen sweeping sand off the number six green with brooms. The course was originally owned and maintained by the County of San Bernardino. It was transferred to the City of Twentynine Palms in 1993 and purchased by the Ficara family in 1997. It is now Roadrunner Dunes.

Knott's Sky Ranch and Motel of the 1940s and 1950s is the site of today's Knott Sky Park. Russell Knott, son of Knott's Berry Farm founders Walter and Cordelia Knott, came to the desert in 1939 to cure his asthma. He returned after World War II, built a runway and five motel rooms on 40 acres, and entertained friends who flew in for weekends. In 1959, Knott donated the land to the water district, who leased it to the City of Twentynine Palms in 1964.

The nation's foremost wildflower painter, Henry R. Mockel, made Twentynine Palms his home. The German-born artist and botanical illustrator with his wife, Beverly, opened Pioneer Art Gallery in the Plaza in 1961 (later called Henry R. Mockel Studio). Mockel was famous for his published book, *Mockel's Desert Flower Notebook*. His oil paintings, watercolors, and serigraphs of desert flora were exhibited extensively, and many are in permanent national collections. (Courtesy of Rosemary Brockway.)

The Weed Show is Twentynine Palms' most unusual event. In July 1940, American printmaker Mildred Bryant Brooks of Pasadena came to deliver a lecture to the Twentynine Palms Women's Club. When the women apologized for not having any flowers for the table, she suggested they use native plant material. Mary Hayes and Ada Hatch went outdoors and collected some desert weeds. Mildred's ensuing demonstration on artistic weed compositions inspired the annual judged competition that has run since 1941.

Celebrating the 12th anniversary of the Twentynine Palms Artists' Guild are from left to right, *Los Angeles Times* columnist Ed Ainsworth, Lee Lukes Pickering, Barbara Hilton, actor and writer Will Rogers Jr., and artist John W. Hilton. The guild was formed in 1951 by Merritt Boyer, John Hilton (founding president), Evelyn Hutchinson, Michael Malloy, Kirk Martin, Vera Martin, Edna Onderdonk, and Fritiof Perssons. (Photograph by Burton Frasher.)

Actor James Cagney (left), seen sketching his artistic mentor, John Hilton, had a desert retreat in Twentynine Palms for many years. Although somewhat reclusive after first retiring from show business in the early 1960s, Cagney was developing his talents as a sketch artist and painter and enjoyed spending creative time with his friend Hilton, renowned desert artist. They frequently attended gallery receptions and local gatherings together. (Photograph by Burton Frasher.)

The Charlton adobe served as the Twentynine Palms Artists' Guild's gallery from 1956 to 1963. Designed by landscape architect Gerald W. Charlton and built in 1933–1934 by the Stubbs brothers, it was the first house in the early Twentynine Palms Corporation subdivision. In 1967, widower Charlton married widow Irene Zimmers, a watercolor artist, who lived in the adobe until her death in 1997. It is now part of 29 Palms Inn.

Western novelist Tom J. Hopkins hired the Stubbs brothers to build this adobe just east of the 29 Palms Inn in 1936. It was the second house built in the Twentynine Palms Corporation subdivision. Later owners Mr. and Mrs. Sam Stocking offered the adobe to the artists' guild in 1963. To this day, the historic adobe remains the home of Twentynine Palms Art Gallery and Gift Shop.

Harold and Lucile Weight were prolific writers of more than 500 articles on the Desert Southwest, many of them in *Desert Magazine* and the *Desert Trail* newspaper. In 1949, they published *Calico Print*, chronicling desert history. They spent many years traveling and interviewing the few remaining prospectors and residents of old mining camps. The Weights lived in Twentynine Palms for 46 years. (Courtesy of Dennis G. Casebier.)

Enjoying a desert afternoon on writer Adelaide Arnold's patio in 1946 are, from left to right, Harry Holt, Walter Ketchum, Adelaide Arnold, Ada T., Elizabeth, and mother Ada Hatch. Arnold was a prolific writer who lived in Twentynine Palms from the late-1930s to the late-1960s. Her stories, poetry, and articles appeared in numerous magazines, including the *Atlantic Monthly*.

A banner headline on the front page of the *Desert Trail* on Thursday, November 5, 1987, announced victory for incorporation of this desert community, which would become formally known on November 23, 1987, as the City of Twentynine Palms. Cityhood supporters all over town awaited the election results, and this group at the 29 Palms Inn made the front page. Rejoicing at the bar on election night, November 3, after receiving good news from the San Bernardino County Registrar of Voters office are, from left to right, John Masterson, Owen Gillick, and Jane Grunt Smith. Out of 14 candidates running for the first city council in 1987, those elected to lead the city were Charles W. "Chuck" Bell (mayor), Christopher J. Dobler, Jeffrey B. Dunn, Lester W. Krushat, and Frederick A. "Fred" Libby. (Photograph by Deborah Hall, the *Desert Trail*.)

Discover Thousands of Local History Books
Featuring Millions of Vintage Images

Arcadia Publishing, the leading local history publisher in the United States, is committed to making history accessible and meaningful through publishing books that celebrate and preserve the heritage of America's people and places.

Find more books like this at
www.arcadiapublishing.com

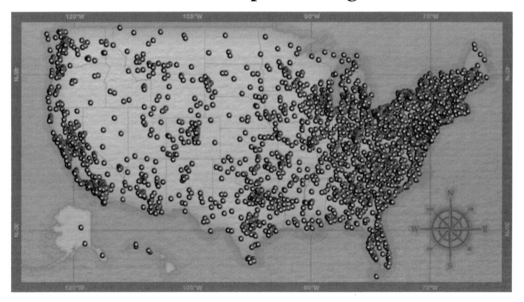

Search for your hometown history, your old stomping grounds, and even your favorite sports team.